THE AMAZING HARRY KELLAR

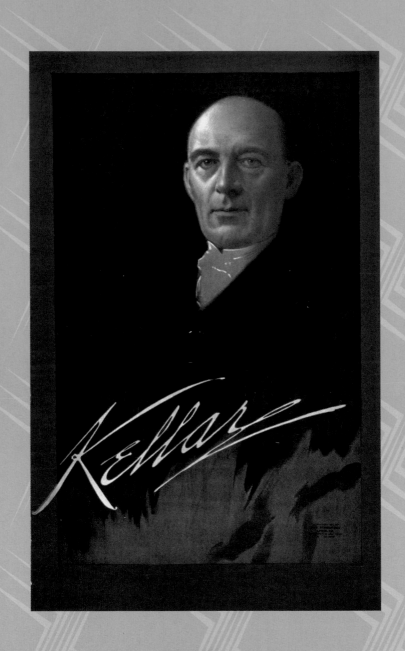

THE MAGICIAN
HARRY KELLAR, 1902

THE AMAZING
HARRY KELLAR

GREAT AMERICAN
MAGICIAN

Gail Jarrow

CALKINS CREEK
Honesdale, Pennsylvania

*For information
about permission to reproduce
selections from this book,
please contact
permissions@highlights.com.*

Calkins Creek
An Imprint of
Boyds Mills Press, Inc.
815 Church Street
Honesdale, Pennsylvania 18431

Printed in China

ISBN: 978-1-59078-865-3

Library of Congress
Control Number: 2011940465

First edition

10 9 8 7 6 5 4 3 2 1

Designed by
Bill Anton I Service Station
Production by
Margaret Mosomillo

Titles set in
Agency Open, Blackoak, Impact,
Linoscript, and Madrone
Text set in
Egyptienne and Trade Gothic

FOR KYLE AND LAUREN,
WHO KNOW A THING
OR TWO
ABOUT BRINGING MAGIC
TO THE STAGE

Acknowledgments

WITH GREAT appreciation, I tip my hat to those who helped me transform an idea into a book:

Lisa and Rich Gensheimer, documentary filmmakers of Main Street Media, who opened the curtain and introduced me to Harry Kellar. They directed my attention toward the best resources, provided thoughtful feedback on the manuscript, and lent a hand whenever I asked.

Mike Caveney, magician and historian, who shared his time, considerable knowledge, and amazing Kellar images. I'm grateful for Mike's careful reading of the manuscript and excellent suggestions. Without his generous assistance, I could not have pulled off this trick.

Harry Kellar "Ted" Blakely, Kellar's great-great-nephew, who was born on the magician's birthday. Ted's family stories captured the spirit of his remarkable relative.

Bill Miesel, magician and author, whose years of detective work revealed forgotten details of Kellar's life. His comments on my manuscript were invaluable.

Clark Evans and the staff at the Library of Congress Rare Books and Special Collections Reading Room, who helped me uncover a few secrets myself.

Bill Anton | Service Station, Juanita Galuska, Jeryl Genschow, Robbin Gourley, and Joan Hyman, who worked their magic behind the scenes.

And Carolyn P. Yoder, who deserves an extra nod. Her editorial skills combine the eye of a critic and the encouragement of a friendly audience.

—*GJ*

Contents

READING THE BOOK OF MAGIC, 1894

Kellar gets help with his magic from the devil and two imps. (See a similar poster on pages 88–89.)

THE MAGIC
POSTERS

BEFORE his magic show arrived in a town, Harry Kellar hired men to glue his advertising posters onto buildings and fences. For most of his career, Kellar ordered his posters from Strobridge Lithographing Company of Ohio and New York. The examples featured in this book were designed and printed by Strobridge, unless otherwise noted.

Posters often featured a Kellar illusion. Many showed him with little devils, or imps. People once thought that a magician's power came from the devil or the spirit world. Kellar played on that superstition to make his illusions and tricks seem more mysterious.

Strobridge printed the posters using stone lithography. An artist created a painting on flat limestone blocks. Then the art was transferred to paper.

Today a Kellar poster sells for thousands of dollars.

THE SHRINE OF KOOMRA-SAMI, 1895

When Kellar performed this illusion, his male assistant stepped inside a cage and the cage curtains closed.
The curtains flew open again. The man had multiplied, and the cage now held him, his double, and a young girl.

PRESENTING...
HARRY KELLAR!

THE FIRST AMERICAN-BORN MAGICIAN TO GAIN WORLDWIDE CELEBRITY.

IN 1900, Americans loved magic shows, and their favorite magician was Harry Kellar. Kellar's stage performances sold out as people lined up to see his latest breathtaking illusion. His face and reputation were known everywhere. He traveled to five continents and became the first American-born magician to gain worldwide celebrity.

Harry Kellar is still admired by today's magicians. But most people have never heard of him. Instead, they think of Harry Houdini as America's greatest magician. Yet Kellar was born in America, and Houdini was not. Kellar was a more talented magician whose career lasted longer than Houdini's. In fact, Houdini idolized Kellar, who was twenty-five years Houdini's senior.

Why has Houdini's fame lasted, though Kellar's has faded?

Houdini was a better escape artist than magician and a better self-promoter than anyone else. He made himself a superstar. At the peak of his career in 1926, Houdini died unexpectedly, shocking the world and guaranteeing that he would not be forgotten.

Harry Kellar was a more modest man. He impressed the public by demonstrating his conjuring skills and exceptional showmanship. He thrilled and amazed audiences with his illusions, while capturing their affections. He encouraged other magicians and advanced the popularity of stage magic.

Kellar achieved his fame slowly during a career that lasted almost half a century. This is the story of his lifetime of hard work, determination, and . . . adventure.

HARRY HOUDINI
(1874–1926)

Houdini was born as Ehrich Weiss in Budapest, Hungary. He grew up in Wisconsin and New York. At the age of seventeen, he began working as a magician, basing his stage name on the famous French magician Jean Eugène Robert-Houdin. In his early twenties, Houdini developed an escape act in which he freed himself from ropes, handcuffs, and straitjackets. By 1900, Houdini had become an international star known for his daring escapes. He first met Harry Kellar in 1908, at the end of Kellar's career. The two later became good friends. When Houdini was fifty-two, he died after his appendix ruptured.

[LEFT]
Jean Eugène Robert-Houdin
(1805–1871)
Originally a clockmaker, Robert-Houdin turned his talents to magic.

[ABOVE]
Houdini's Milk-Can Escape
Houdini, wearing handcuffs, prepares to be locked into a milk can filled with water. Thrilling escape tricks like this one made Houdini a star.

[OPPOSITE]
Houdini's Water-Torture Cell
In one of his most sensational escapes, Houdini was sealed upside down inside a water-filled cabinet.

KELLAR STROLLS, 1900

Kellar always performed in evening clothes, which made him look elegant and classy.

THE WIZARD
CASTS HIS SPELL

ON A SUNNY Saturday afternoon in January 1904, President Theodore Roosevelt took his four youngest children to see America's most famous magician. The First Family clapped as Harry Kellar entered the stage of Washington's Lafayette Theatre. The wizard was dressed in stylish evening clothes.

The Great Kellar asked to borrow six rings from his audience. The president's twelve-year-old daughter, Ethel, handed over her new turquoise ring. She and her three brothers watched wide-eyed as the magician crushed the six rings with a hammer.

When the pieces were small enough, Kellar jammed them into the barrel of his pistol. He aimed the gun across the stage at a finely crafted wooden box. Then he fired, startling the audience.

With a flourish, the magician opened the box. Inside was a second box. Inside that one was a third. When Kellar finally opened the sixth box, he pulled out a bouquet of rosebuds. The borrowed rings were attached to the bouquet by ribbons. Ethel was relieved that her ring hadn't been smashed.

Smiling, Kellar returned each ring to its owner—except Ethel. She turned to her father. "Papa, I didn't get my ring back. Tell that man I want my ring."

To her dismay, the president said nothing as the magician went on to a trick creating American flags from yellow tissue paper.

Next Kellar produced a large, dark glass bottle. He offered several audience members the beverage of their choice. As he poured from the bottle, water flowed into one person's glass, wine into another, and whiskey into another.

When the bottle was empty, Kellar suddenly seemed to remember Ethel Roosevelt. He apologized to her for losing her ring. Maybe he could look for it in the bottle, he said. The wizard grabbed a hammer and broke the bottle. Inside was a white guinea pig. Tied to a blue ribbon around its neck was Ethel Roosevelt's turquoise ring.

Kellar brought the squealing, squirming guinea pig to the president's daughter. "Would you like to keep it for a pet?" he asked.

Ethel nodded enthusiastically.

"You shall have it, seeing that I lost your ring, and came so near not finding it."

Kellar deftly wrapped paper around the guinea pig and gave it back to Ethel. When she removed the paper, the guinea pig was gone! In its place she found a bouquet of pink roses.

The audience applauded.

But Ethel's older brother Kermit was disappointed. "Shucks," he said, "I thought it was the guinea pig."

The great magician Harry Kellar had amazed his audience again.

IMPISH FRIENDS, 1894

Kellar's helpers whisper magical secrets.

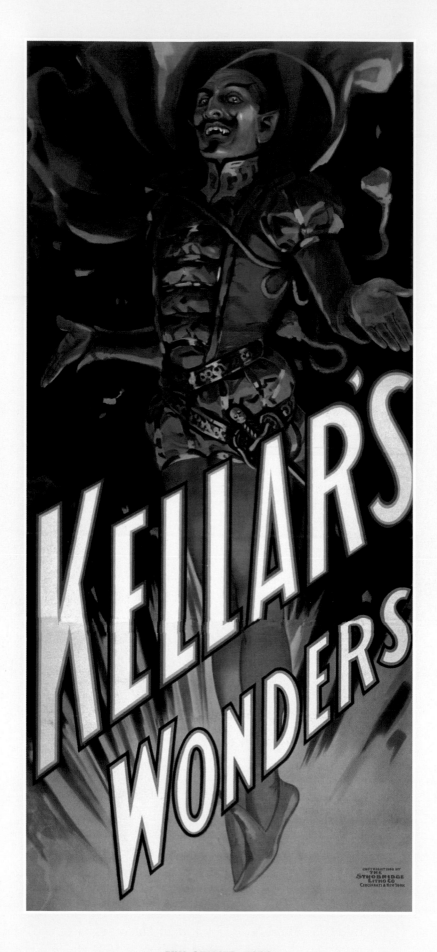

EVIL SPIRITS, 1900

Kellar's posters often hinted at a connection between magic and evil.

THE OPENING TRICK

THE MAGIC began in a Pennsylvania town on the shore of Lake Erie. On July 11, 1849, Harry Kellar entered the world as Heinrich Keller. He was the first in his family to be born an American.

Two years before, his parents—Franz and Catherine Keller—traveled by ship across the Atlantic Ocean from their birthplace in Germany. Like them, hundreds of thousands of Germans fled to the United States during the middle of the nineteenth century. In Germany, people couldn't find jobs, houses, or enough food. The immigrants hoped to make a better life for themselves in America.

KELLAR'S BIRTHPLACE

Harry Kellar was born in this house in Erie, Pennsylvania. He had an older brother and sister. Kellar remained close to his brother, Eduard, throughout his life. There is no record of his sister, Regina, past childhood.

After landing in New York City, the Kellers and their toddler son and infant daughter headed for Erie, Pennsylvania. About five thousand people lived in the town, including a large German population. The Kellers had heard that there were plenty of jobs.

Business was booming thanks to the opening of a new canal that connected Erie with the city of Pittsburgh and major railroads to the south.

Frank Keller—as he now called himself—found a job as an unskilled laborer. Later he sold fish he caught in Lake Erie and laid brick for new buildings. He worked long hours to support his family.

The Kellers' third child, Heinrich, or Henry, was born during their second summer in America. Henry's early life wasn't always easy. By the time he was seven, his mother had died and his father had remarried.

Henry was happiest when he was out of the house, fishing in Erie's harbor or helping in his neighbor's garden. He liked excitement, too. He and his friends made a game of sprinting across the tracks in front of fast-moving trains. They competed to see who could get closest to the train as the engineer blew the warning whistle.

EXPLOSION

Frank Keller was determined that his spirited son would learn a trade. When Henry was ten years old, his father apprenticed him to a local druggist.

But being stuck inside preparing drugs was boring for Henry. To amuse himself, he sometimes mixed chemicals to see what would happen. One day his mixture exploded, damaging the store. Henry needed no more proof "that the drug business was neither healthful nor profitable" for a boy like him.

With both the druggist and his father furious at him, Henry jumped on a freight train and skipped town. He hopped off a hundred miles away in the next big city—Cleveland, Ohio.

Being alone in an unfamiliar city would frighten most eleven-year-olds. Not Henry. It didn't take him long to find jobs at a newspaper printing press and a dry-goods store. In 1860, no laws stopped an employer from hiring a young boy to do adult work.

Cleveland wasn't exciting enough for Henry, though. He jumped on another train, this one on its way to New York City, about five hundred miles to the east. Soon Henry was selling newspapers at a street corner in Lower Manhattan. He talked a hotel night porter into letting him sleep in the hotel's office in exchange for helping to clean up.

MAGIC

One day while Henry was selling his papers, a minister struck up a conversation. The man was impressed by Henry's outgoing personality and sharp mind. He offered to give the boy a home and a tutor who would educate him for the ministry. It sounded like a good deal to Henry. He quit the newsboy business and moved to the minister's home in Canandaigua, halfway across New York State.

NEWSBOY

At the age of eleven, Henry Keller sold newspapers on a corner in New York City, much like this boy from the late 1800s. After he became famous, the magician Harry Kellar performed a free show for newsboys. He told them, "Every American who has attained success has reached it only by hard work against difficulties."

MAGIC'S HISTORY

For thousands of years, magicians in all parts of the world performed amazing feats. In earlier times, magic seemed so mysterious and strange that many people believed it was supernatural. For example, in Europe during the Middle Ages, magic was thought to be the work of witches and evil spirits.

As time went on, people in most places saw magic as entertainment. Magicians performed on streets and at fairs. By the late eighteenth century, they appeared on stages, too. Magic shows often included more than sleight-of-hand tricks. Some performers added juggling, fire-eating, tumbling, fortune-telling, mind reading, ventriloquism, or automatons, which were mechanical figures that behaved like humans.

In the early American colonies, magic performances were outlawed by leaders. They were suspicious of magic and considered it a sinful waste of time. Gradually, laws changed. In 1734, a German-born magician gave the first known colonial magic show, in New York City. By the second half of the 1700s, magicians—mostly from Europe—were touring America.

When Harry Kellar was born in 1849, magic shows were familiar to Americans. The top magicians were European and performed in the larger cities of the East, South, and Midwest. They appeared in theaters that were also used for operas, plays, and concerts. The less famous traveling magicians presented their shows at small halls or fairs, the way conjurers had for centuries.

Mᴿ PHILIPPE.
Physicien Chinois.

Imp. d Aubert & Cⁱᵉ

The Magician Wizard
This 1839 illustration shows the wizard robes worn by magicians at that time. A few years later, Jean Eugène Robert-Houdin performed in formal evening clothes, introducing the style adopted by Kellar and other magicians of the late nineteenth century.

Sometime later, the minister treated Henry to a magic show in Penn Yan, a nearby town. The magician called himself the Fakir of Ava. Henry was mesmerized as the Fakir turned pieces of paper into coffee, sugar, and milk. Each of the Fakir's tricks was better than the one before.

At that moment, Henry "got the urge to go on the stage." Fascinated by what he'd seen, he began reading books about magic. Although the minister had been kind to him, Henry realized that he wasn't cut out to be a preacher. He "wanted liberty, freedom; he wanted to see the world."

It was time to move on again.

THE LUCKY DOG

Making his way westward back toward Lake Erie, Henry found a job doing farm chores. He still held on to his dream of becoming a magician. When he spotted a want ad in a newspaper from Buffalo, New York, he saw his chance. The same magician who had sparked his interest in magic—the Fakir of Ava—was advertising for an assistant.

The Fakir, whose real name was Isaiah Harris Hughes, lived outside of Buffalo. Henry immediately set out to apply for the job in person.

As he approached the conjurer's weathered fence, Henry took a deep breath. He was a little afraid of the mysterious magician. But he desperately wanted the job. He pushed open Hughes's gate and entered the yard.

Suddenly, a barking black-and-tan dog bounded toward him. Wagging its tail, the dog jumped up on Henry.

Hughes came to the door and called out, "Every other boy that has come here has been attacked by that dog; you are the first he has welcomed."

The magician had found the perfect assistant. He figured that a boy who easily makes friends with animals could win over a human audience, too. He motioned to Henry. "Come in; you are engaged."

Thanks to Fake, the Fakir's dog, young Henry Keller's life in magic was about to begin.

FLOATING ON AIR, 1894

Eye-catching posters of Kellar's magical levitation drew audiences to his shows.

THE MAGICIAN'S APPRENTICE

HENRY KELLER and Isaiah Hughes, the Fakir of Ava, headed out on their magic tour. They traveled from town to town by train, horse-drawn coaches, and wagons. Hughes had performed for years throughout the United States, and he knew the best places to make money. But because the Civil War was raging in the South, he and Henry toured only in the Northern states.

THE FAKIR OF AVA (1813?–1891)

Isaiah Harris Hughes based his stage name on Ava, a city in Burma (also known as Myanmar). But Hughes (on the right) was born in England, not Burma, and he wasn't a fakir. He knew that his magic act would seem more mystical and exotic to audiences if he pretended to be from a far-off country. Kellar later said that Hughes was "one of my best and truest friends." This photograph was taken in 1885 when Hughes came to see Kellar (left) perform in Philadelphia.

For a boy in his early teens, life on the road was exciting. Hughes taught his assistant the art of magic as well as the way to move and act onstage. Henry also learned how to think on his feet when a trick went wrong.

Before long, he had the chance to put his lessons to the test. During one performance, the Fakir of Ava asked someone in the audience to donate a watch. Then he seemed to smash the watch and load its pieces into a pistol.

Actually, the magician slipped the watch to Henry, who secretly hooked it onto the back of a target. The trick was supposed to work so that when the Fakir fired his pistol, a device on the bull's-eye flipped the watch to the front of the target. The audience would believe that the Fakir had magically put the watch back together as he shot it onto the bull's-eye.

But just as the Fakir prepared to shoot, Henry noticed that the bull's-eye device was broken. He couldn't fix it to flip around, and he couldn't signal the magician.

With quick hands, Henry snatched the watch. Hurrying into the audience, he shouted that he had an emergency telegram to deliver. While he walked up the aisle calling a name he had made up, Henry dropped the watch into an unsuspecting man's pocket.

The Fakir realized what his young assistant was doing. Up on the stage, the magician spun a fantastic story about where the missing watch had gone. Finally, he pointed to the man on the aisle. "Look in your pocket, sir," he urged.

When the surprised man pulled out the watch, the crowd applauded. Henry had saved the trick.

GOING IT ALONE

In his spare time, Henry practiced his magic skills. Once he mastered a trick, he continued to practice until he could do it without thinking. Even small tricks took hours of repetition before his hands moved automatically.

Gradually, Henry gained confidence. Starting at age sixteen, he performed occasional shows by himself. When he was eighteen, he felt ready to go out on his own. The Fakir gave him some magic equipment, and Henry hit the road. He called himself *Harry Keller*.

Harry Keller failed to attract crowds in the halls and theaters of small midwestern towns. His hands were too clumsy to *excel* at sleight of hand. His poor grammar made him seem unsophisticated and uneducated. Besides that, Harry picked an unfortunate time to start his solo career. The country was recovering from the Civil War. People had little money to spend on magic shows.

In 1869, with his prospects looking dim, Harry found new hope in La Crosse, Wisconsin. The famous Davenport Brothers were performing at a local theater. Recognizing a good opportunity, Harry convinced the Davenports to hire him as an assistant.

THE SPIRIT CABINET

Ira and William Davenport were known in America and Europe for their Spirit Cabinet, a large wooden box with doors across the front. The brothers sat far apart on benches inside the cabinet. Volunteers from the audience bound their hands and tied the brothers tightly to the benches. Their assistants placed bells and a tambourine, trumpet, and guitar in the center of the cabinet.

TRICKS AND ILLUSIONS

The art of magic involves performing tricks and illusions to captivate an audience. A magician's *trick* is small enough to hold in his hands. Kellar was performing a trick when he shot Ethel Roosevelt's ring from a pistol and it ended up around a guinea pig's neck. In a stage *illusion*, something happens to a person or big animal. The magician usually uses large props and equipment. When Harry Kellar floated a woman in the air, he was performing an illusion.

As soon as the doors closed, the audience heard the musical instruments playing inside the cabinet. Suddenly, hands reached through the hole at the top of one of the doors. The trumpet and bells flew out of the opening. In the dim light of theater gas lamps, the scene was eerie.

When an assistant opened the cabinet doors, the brothers were still tied to their separate benches. The audience was stunned. Because the cabinet sat above the floor on supports, people saw that no one could get in or out except through the front doors. Who—or what—had caused the uproar inside the cabinet?

Ira and William Davenport led the audience to believe that ghost hands performed the tricks and played the instruments. The Davenports suggested that because of their special power as mediums, spirits communicated through them. The public was fascinated by spiritualism and communicating with the dead. The Davenports' show attracted big audiences.

Harry discovered the truth about the cabinet. The Davenports had a secret for rapidly escaping from the ropes, no matter how tightly they were knotted. When the doors closed, each man freed himself. The "ghost" hands belonged to the brothers.

For four years, Harry worked with the Davenports and their partner, William Fay. He managed the box office income, handled expenses, and organized their tours. The Davenports' show traveled all over the United States by train. The Transcontinental Railroad had been completed in 1869, and new rail lines were constantly being built.

But Harry gained something even more valuable than business experience during his years with the Davenports. He learned how to do the brothers' rope escape.

THE SPIRIT CABINET

The Davenport brothers (Ira on the far left, William on the far right) pose for a photograph with their Spirit Cabinet. William Fay (1839–1921) is second from the left. The other man is an assistant named Cooper.

In this old print, the brothers are tied up inside the cabinet. An audience volunteer sits between the brothers to verify that the Davenports don't move from their benches and that no one else enters the cabinet. When the doors shut, musical instruments played. A tambourine landed on the volunteer's head. Hands touched his face. When the doors opened, the perplexed volunteer insisted that the brothers never moved inside the dark cabinet. The audience was certain that ghosts had performed the tricks. Actually, the Davenports escaped from their ropes and caused the mischief. Then they slipped their hands back into the knots before the cabinet doors reopened.

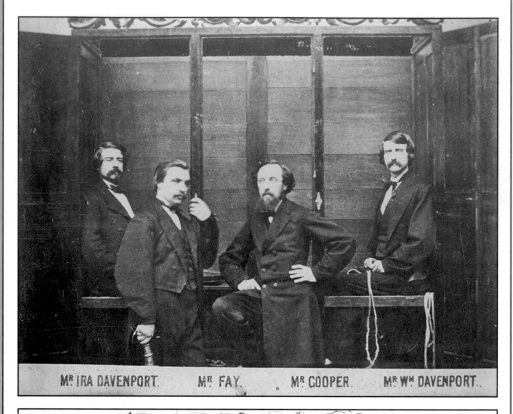

MR IRA DAVENPORT.   MR FAY.   MR COOPER.   MR WM DAVENPORT.

SPIRITUALISM

*I*n 1848, two young sisters from upstate New York, Margaret and Kate Fox, claimed that they received messages from the dead. Within months, thousands of people in America and England were convinced that spirits communicated with the living. This belief is called spiritualism.

Spiritualists think that a person with special power, called a medium, can contact the spirits during a séance. The spirits supposedly send their messages to the living by using the medium's voice, writing on slates, or making rapping sounds. They tip the séance table and make objects fly around the room.

People flocked to mediums throughout Harry Kellar's lifetime, desperate to talk to dead loved ones, including the many soldiers killed in the Civil War (1861–1865), the Spanish-American War (1898), and World War I (1914–1918). Kellar thought that mediums fooled people and made money off their grief. In his show, he proved that he could do all of the tricks that mediums claimed were performed by spirits.

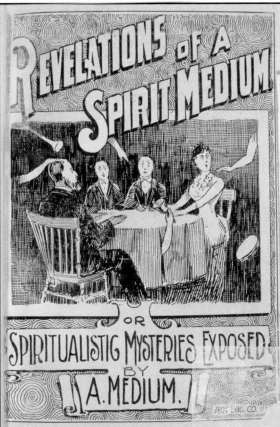

[ABOVE]
Séance, Early 1900s
To make items "float" during a séance, mediums used tricks such as a stick to hold a tambourine above the table.

[LEFT]
Mediums Exposed, 1891
Spirit hands appear at a séance on the title page of a book that exposed the methods used by mediums to fool people.

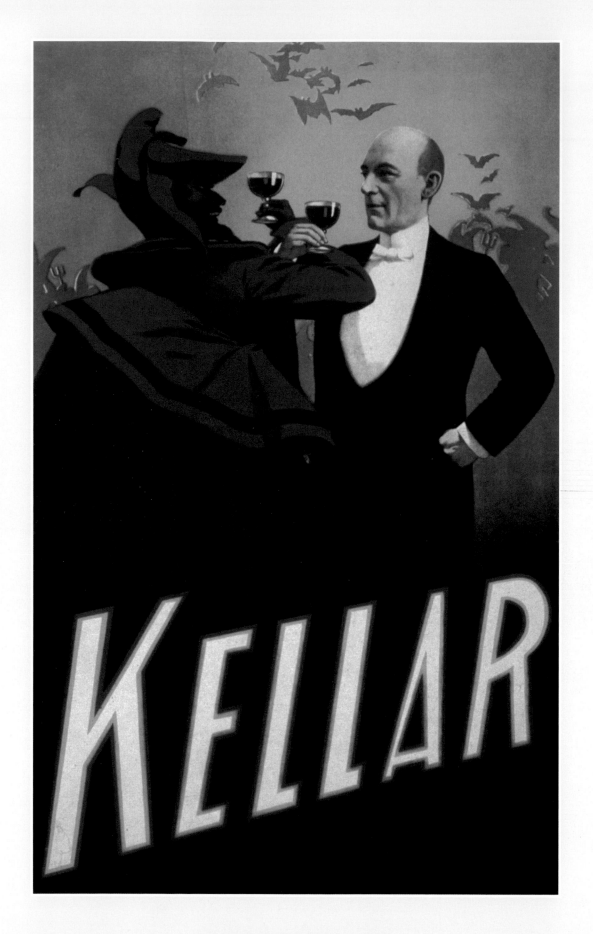

"IN LEAGUE WITH THE DEVIL," 1899

Kellar shares a toast with a devilish figure as other devils carry pitchforks in the background.
Bats, the symbol of demons and spirits, swoop overhead.

"IN LEAGUE WITH THE DEVIL"

BY SPRING 1873, twenty-three-year-old Harry had grown restless managing the Davenport Brothers. He and his co-worker William Fay decided they could make more money with their own show. The two left the Davenports and became "Fay and Keller."

They already had a crowd-pleaser—the Spirit Cabinet. Harry had learned how to escape from knotted ropes in seconds, the key to baffling audiences. Fay and Keller added some small tricks to their performance and were all set to go on tour with a full evening show.

After testing it out in Canada, they moved into the southern United States. By December 1873, the partners had opened in Cuba.

KELLAR'S SPIRIT CABINET

Throughout his career, Harry Kellar used this wooden cabinet, based on the one owned by the Davenport Brothers.

SPANISH PATTER

Harry knew that people enjoyed watching magic even if the magician didn't say a word. But he realized that his performance could be more entertaining if he used patter, or continuous talk. The patter took everyone's attention away from the secret of the trick. It created an atmosphere of mystery and held the audience's interest.

Unfortunately, the Spanish-speaking audiences in Cuba couldn't understand a single word of Harry's English patter. To solve this problem, he first tried to use an interpreter onstage. But his show became bogged down by the constant interruptions needed to translate his patter. Harry was also concerned that the man might interpret his words incorrectly or interfere with his magic.

707 BROADWAY,

Next, he asked someone to write out his patter in Spanish so that he could memorize it. This worked well. His Spanish, he later explained, "was good enough to make every person in the audience understand him, and . . . at times bad enough to be very funny."

Harry discovered that he had a knack for languages. His performances were stronger when he spoke like his audience.

After sailing from Cuba, Fay and Keller spent eighteen months touring large towns and cities in Mexico, Central America, and South America. Many of the people had never seen a magic show like theirs before.

When they were lucky, the partners traveled by train or steamship. Frequently, they had to journey over rugged roads on a stagecoach, wagon, or the back of a mule. Because bandits tried to rob travelers, Harry carried a rifle and a revolver.

**THE MAGICIAN
IN HIS LATE TWENTIES**

Harry had light brown hair and blue eyes. Newspaper reporters described him as a tall man.

The two magicians found that it was too expensive to haul the Spirit Cabinet everywhere. Instead, they hired people to build it in each town they visited. The audience was even more amazed by the show because local carpenters had made the ordinary cabinet.

Fay and Keller told audiences that the sounds and objects coming from within the cabinet were part of a magic trick. Unlike the Davenport Brothers, they made it clear that no ghosts or spirits were involved.

Some people didn't believe the magicians. They were sure that spirits created the commotion inside the cabinet. In Argentina, officials stopped Harry from performing because, they said, he was connected to evil. In Mexico City, newspapers charged him with being "in league with the devil."

That kind of publicity sold more tickets. Wherever they went, Fay and Keller filled the theaters. Even the emperor of Brazil, Dom Pedro II, came to their show several times.

TRAVEL TROUBLE

Harry enjoyed seeing a different part of the world. But even for someone who had spent years touring the United States, travel in foreign countries was a challenge.

In Mexico, the chili peppers in the food made Harry feel as if he were "eating fire." In Peru, he was served a tasty dish made with a sweet, tender meat. When he asked what it was, his host told him it was cooked guinea pig. Harry was sorry to hear that. He used guinea pigs in his tricks and was fond of them—alive.

Harry encountered new illnesses, too. In early 1875, when he was twenty-five, he caught yellow fever, a disease spread by mosquitoes. From Uruguay, he wrote his father back in Erie, Pennsylvania: "I have been very sick for the past three weeks. . . . I am all skin and bones and as yellow as if painted. . . . Your Affectionate Son, Henry."

At the end of July 1875, Fay and Keller decided to end their successful South American tour and take their show to Europe. They boarded an ocean steamer bound for England. In their luggage, the magicians carried their profits—thousands of dollars worth of gold and silver coins and diamonds.

Three weeks later, the ship had crossed the Atlantic Ocean and reached the coast of France. Then in a thick fog, the steamer hit the rocks. Two people were killed in the shipwreck.

Harry and William escaped, but their props, costumes, and treasure sank with the steamer. Harry made it to shore with only the diamond ring on his finger and the clothes on his back.

Needing cash, he contacted the bank in New York where he kept his savings. He was shocked to find that the bank had failed. In those days, bank deposits weren't insured by the government. His money was gone.

A disheartened Harry sent his father a short note: "I am too feeble to write, but hope to see you soon."

PERPLEXING CABINET, 1894

Ghosts, skeletons, and
devilish imps
help Kellar assemble his
Spirit Cabinet.

MAGIC FROM EGYPT, 1888

Kellar created an atmosphere of mystery by telling audiences that he learned his magic in the far corners of the world.
This poster has an Egyptian theme, showing the Sphinx, an obelisk, pyramids, and camels.
It was printed by W. J. Morgan & Company of Cleveland, Ohio.

THE FLYING CAGE

HARRY REFUSED to let the shipwreck stop him. Somehow he would replace his magic equipment and get back on the stage. William Fay was less optimistic. He returned to the Davenport Brothers show.

From France, Harry traveled to London, England, to visit Egyptian Hall. Skilled European magicians came to this theater to present their new tricks and illusions. If Harry was going to compete successfully with other magicians, he needed fresh and exciting material. Here was the place to find it.

One trick caught his eye. A magician held a small wire birdcage containing a live canary. One, two, three . . . *Poof!* Suddenly, the birdcage and bird disappeared from his hands. It was a stunning trick—exactly what Harry was looking for.

He sold his diamond ring, bought a duplicate magic birdcage, and headed back to America. Without the inventor's permission, he traded the secret of the birdcage to a maker of magic apparatus in New York City. In return, the man rebuilt Harry's lost equipment.

FAY AND HOUDINI

William Fay (seated) retired from his magic career in 1877 and settled in Australia. Years later, in 1895, Fay and Ira Davenport came out of retirement for a short-lived and unsuccessful revival of their séance act. In 1910, while escape artist Harry Houdini was performing in Australia, Houdini visited Fay, the former partner of his friend Harry Kellar. Houdini wanted to hear about Fay's time with the Davenport brothers, who had also been experts at rope escapes. William Fay died in 1921 at age eighty-one.

JOHN NEVIL MASKELYNE

Maskelyne (1839–1917) was the most well-known British magician of his day and a great inventor of illusions. When he was twenty-five, he saw the Davenport Brothers perform in Great Britain. He and his partner George Cooke (1825–1904) first gained fame by imitating the Davenports' Spirit Cabinet act. Later they established the Home of Mystery at London's Egyptian Hall, where talented magicians appeared. Harry Kellar often visited the magic theater to gather ideas for his own show. Maskelyne's son and grandson became famous magicians, too.

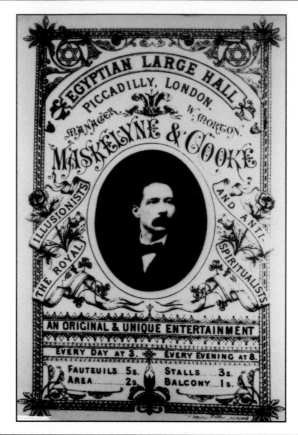

[TOP]
Maskelyne & Cooke
This poster—featuring John Nevil Maskelyne's portrait—advertised Maskelyne & Cooke, described as the Royal Illusionists and Anti-Spiritualists.

[ABOVE]
Egyptian Hall, London
The front of Egyptian Hall, around 1900.

THE ROYAL ILLUSIONISTS

By October 1875, just two months after the shipwreck, Harry was in business again. He found a new partner, A. Litherland Cunard. They called themselves "The Royal Illusionists," a name they copied from the famous British magicians of Egyptian Hall, John Nevil Maskelyne and George Cooke.

Keller and Cunard set out by ship for South America, where Harry had had earlier success. Their show filled an evening with a variety of magical marvels, including Harry's reliable Cabinet Séance and his new Flying Cage. Harry did tricks with flowers and handkerchiefs. He made a guinea pig disappear from a box and reappear in a bottle. He poured glasses of water and wine from the same pitcher.

Unfortunately, the Royal Illusionists had disappointing ticket sales on their tour of South America. They depended on selling enough seats to pay for renting the theater and for their travel and living expenses. When Harry realized that they weren't going to make sufficient money to continue the tour, he canceled the rest of their appearances. The Royal Illusionists would have to take their show where they could count on larger audiences.

Harry shrugged off this failure. He loved magic. He loved performing. He'd find a way to overcome the setback. In June 1876, he wrote his father that ups and downs were part of being a magician. "There is only one road to me for success; that is through energy, 'sticktoitiveness,' and perseverance."

Harry made changes to improve the show. He added two brothers: Ling Look, a sword-swallower and fire-eater, and Yamadeva, an escape artist. After trying out their new program in the western United States, the Royal Illusionists sailed to Australia in late summer 1876. Magic shows were popular in the British colony. Harry hoped for strong ticket sales.

On the way, he changed the spelling of his name to *Kellar*. He didn't want to be confused with the well-known magician Robert Heller, who performed in the United States and around the world.

STARTLING ENTERTAINMENT

For the next eight months, the Royal Illusionists toured Australian cities. The Flying Cage was a sensation. But it sparked protests. In Sydney, Australia's largest city, bird lovers accused Harry of killing a canary each time he did the trick. How else could the bird disappear?

Harry offered to prove to the SPCA (Society for the Prevention of Cruelty to Animals) that he never hurt a single bird. With newspaper reporters watching, two men from the SPCA tied a thread around the canary's leg and placed the bird in Kellar's cage. Harry held the cage in his hands. *Poof!* The cage and canary vanished.

> "THERE IS ONLY ONE ROAD TO ME FOR SUCCESS; THAT IS THROUGH ENERGY, 'STICK-TOITIVENESS,' AND PERSEVERANCE."

Moments later, Kellar produced the canary unharmed, with the thread still on its leg. Thanks to the newspaper publicity, the Royal Illusionists filled the Sydney theater every night after that.

Harry often wrote to his father, brother, and friends in Erie. He sent them stamped envelopes with his current address so that they would write to him—"just to know that you sometimes think of me," he told them.

From Australia, the Royal Illusionists took their show through Asia. In the Dutch colony of Java (now part of Indonesia), Harry was able to make his patter understood because Dutch is similar to

THE ROYAL ILLUSIONISTS, 1876–1877

Kellar performed in the western United States, Australia, and throughout Asia with the brothers Ling Look and Yamadeva.
Their advertising claimed that they had performed at London's famed Egyptian Hall. They had not.

the German he learned from his parents. Kellar performed before the kings of Siam (now Thailand) and Burma. Traveling by steamship, the Royal Illusionists also visited the British colonies of Singapore and Hong Kong.

Moving a magic show from country to country was sometimes slow and difficult. The Royal Illusionists crossed thousands of miles of ocean by steamship and used train lines wherever they existed.

At times, they had to ride on bumpy dirt roads in wagons pulled by oxen. The travelers put up with harsh conditions and illness. Harry was sick for several weeks with another disease spread by mosquitoes, dengue fever.

To Harry, performing in front of an audience was worth all of the effort. In the summer of 1877, shortly before his twenty-eighth birthday, he wrote his father: "I do not think I will see you again for two years. I am making plenty of money where I am and in no particular hurry to return to the States."

Then that autumn during the tour of China, Yamadeva died of a sudden illness. Not long after, his sword-swallowing brother Ling Look developed a fatal liver disease. The grieving Harry struggled to wear a smile and go onstage. "I must fulfill my engagements alone," he wrote his father, "although my heart is heavy as lead."

CHALLENGING THE SPIRITUALISTS

In order to continue the tour, Harry hired two replacements. The new Royal Illusionists spent the next three months in India.

Harry was eager to watch performances by the Indian fakirs, or street magicians. He saw that they didn't possess special powers. In fact, he had performed many of their tricks himself.

After India, Harry and his troupe traveled for four months in the Middle East and Africa. As part of his show, Kellar attacked spiritualists and mediums who claimed to communicate with ghosts during séances.

He publicly announced that he could perform everything that occurred during a séance. To prove that he, not ghosts, created the sounds and commotion inside the Spirit Cabinet, Harry challenged anyone to tie him up before he entered. People filled the theaters to see if he could escape the knots.

In South Africa, a spiritualist used eleven feet of rope to tie Kellar's hands together with sailor's knots. Harry entered the cabinet and the doors were shut. Nearly a minute passed. He usually escaped in seconds. Had Harry Kellar been defeated?

Finally, he opened the cabinet door, completely free of the rope. His escape had been difficult. The tightly knotted rope had cut the skin on his wrists.

"Bravo, Kellar!" shouted the audience.

In another theater, a spiritualist tied Kellar tightly and announced to the audience, "I have trapped the fox."

The minute the man turned his back, Harry slipped a hand from the knot and tapped him on his shoulder. "If you have two of my hands tied behind my back," Kellar said, "I must have been royally endowed by Nature with a third hand."

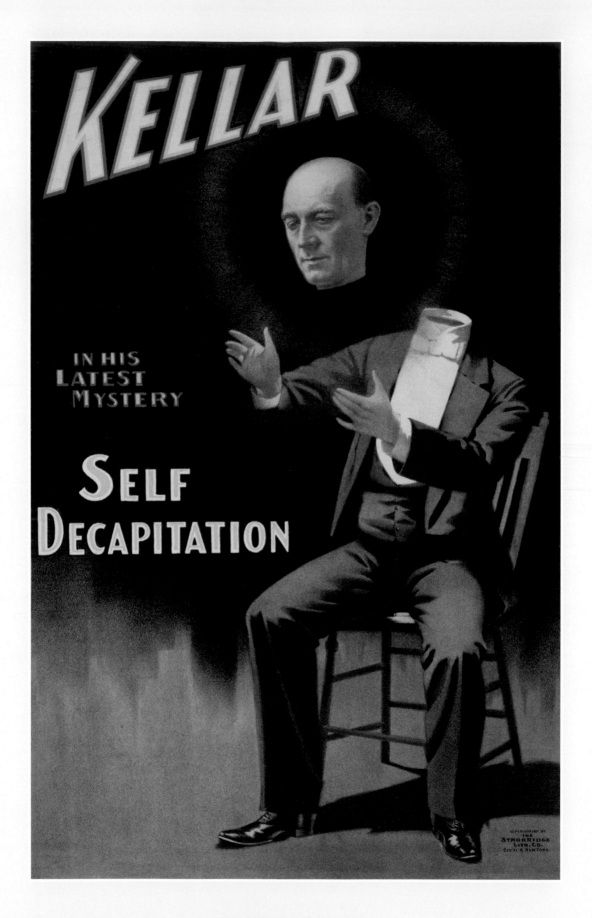

OFF WITH HIS HEAD, 1897

In this illusion, Kellar sat on a chair in the middle of the stage.
While the audience watched—some horrified—he lifted his head from his body.
As his head floated away, it smiled and nodded. Then it disappeared.

PSYCHO

AFTER NEARLY three years of world travel, Harry Kellar returned to London in the summer of 1878. He wanted to see the new magic being performed at Egyptian Hall.

Magician John Nevil Maskelyne had a fantastic addition to his show—an automaton called Psycho. The life-sized mechanical young man was dressed as a Hindu from India. Psycho played cards and shook hands with people. He turned his head and smoked cigarettes. He spelled words by picking up letter cards from a rack. Audience members provided math problems, and Psycho solved them, using number cards to give his answer.

People were intrigued by a robot that could perform such feats. They were even more mystified because Psycho was too small for anyone to work the hands and head from inside. Harry knew this automaton would draw crowds to his show. He hired a maker of magic equipment in England to build him a copy.

**MASKELYNE
WITH HIS PSYCHO**

PSYCHO

When Harry Kellar saw John Nevil Maskelyne's new automaton in 1878, he arranged to have a copy made for his own show. Psycho sat atop a box, which was supported by a clear glass cylinder. The automaton picked cards from the tray in front of him to display his answers to questions.

Several years after he retired from the stage, Kellar gave Psycho to his friend Harry Houdini. In a note dated May 12, 1919, he wrote to Houdini: "It is with genuine pleasure that I present to you this day my little companion and friend of many years, my Automaton Psycho. . . . He never went on strike, never tired and could always be relied upon to do his level best."

Psycho, 1919
Kellar (left) and Harry Houdini watch Psycho perform.

KELLAR'S WONDERS

Back in the United States, the Royal Illusionists introduced their new two-hour program on the East Coast. Harry was the lead performer. The posters advertised Kellar's Wonders, Psycho, and Cabinet Séances. Harry's dream was to become as popular in the United States as he was in other parts of the world. "Should I succeed," he wrote his father, "I will never leave America again."

His plans were dashed in November 1878 when famous magician Robert Heller died suddenly in Philadelphia. Newspaper critics accused Kellar of using a name similar to Heller's in order to boost his own reputation. Harry protested. He produced proof that his given name was Keller and that he had changed it to *Kellar* two years before.

But the damage was done. Many people considered Harry nothing more than a Heller impostor. Ticket sales plummeted. Harry realized that the Royal Illusionists would have to return to countries where he'd been successful before. In the spring of 1879, the troupe left America on a world tour that would last five years.

Their debut in South America was a hit. They performed in Brazil before large audiences that included their fan Emperor Dom Pedro II. In only two weeks, the Royal Illusionists earned thousands of dollars. During the next three months, they took their show to Uruguay and Argentina.

Now that he had cash to buy new magic equipment, Harry again headed across the ocean to London's Egyptian Hall. Maskelyne had just introduced three new automatons, and Harry wanted them. Just as he had done with Psycho, he paid a man to make copies.

One automaton was a girl who sketched the faces of celebrities suggested by the audience. Kellar called her Clio. A male automaton, which he named Echo, played the cornet. The second male, Phono, played the euphonium, an instrument similar to the tuba.

"A NIGHT IN DREAMLAND"

With Clio, Echo, and Phono added to the show, the Royal Illusionists toured England and Scotland. "A Night in Dreamland" included Harry's tried-and-true tricks, the automatons, and the Cabinet Séance. The show brought in big audiences and earned glowing reviews from the British theater critics. One wrote: "There is no one possessing a wider popularity than Kellar." The highlight of the yearlong tour of Great Britain was the April 1880 performance at Queen Victoria's private estate in Scotland.

From Britain, Harry and his company continued their world tour, performing in South Africa, India, Australia, New Zealand, Japan, China, and Siam. Kellar impressed audiences with his Flying Cage and the automatons. In New Zealand, a newspaper raved about the Royal Illusionists: "Their entertainment is certainly entitled to rank foremost of any of the kind ever witnessed here."

In Hong Kong, a reviewer wrote: "The repeated applause . . . was a sure sign that the audience [was] well satisfied with the expert and dexterous manner in which they were being deceived."

Harry enjoyed visiting these countries, meeting new people, and learning their languages. In May 1882, he met nineteen-year-old Eva Medley in Melbourne, Australia, when she came backstage to get his autograph. Harry liked her and promised to send her postcards as he traveled. She promised to write back. For the next five years, they corresponded.

During the world tour, some members of the Royal Illusionists left the troupe, and new ones were hired. Kellar bought out his current partner, John Hodgkins, and became sole owner of the show.

Harry remained the star, and newspapers focused on him. One South African reviewer said of the Cabinet Séance: "The speedy manner in which Mr. Kellar released himself from his rope bonds, literally astonished the beholder."

In Japan, Kellar received praise: "Gifted with a gentlemanly manner, pleasant voice, and fluent and correct delivery, he at once impresses his visitors favorably."

Early in 1884, Harry sailed back to the United States after five years of circling the globe. By the age of thirty-four, he had made the name *Harry Kellar* famous on five continents. Confident of his magic skills and his showmanship, Harry was ready to become the most well-known magician in his own country.

EVA MEDLEY (1862–1910)

While performing in Melbourne, Australia, in 1882, Kellar met Eva Medley. She played cornet with the Melbourne Symphony.

THE COMPETITION

Harry Kellar wasn't the only performer touring the world in the 1870s and 1880s. In South America and Mexico, he and William Fay encountered rival magicians from local cities as well as from Spain. In Asia, Kellar and the Royal Illusionists competed against other live shows, including an American circus and a traveling opera company.

Many magicians performed throughout Continental Europe, perhaps one reason Kellar didn't take his show there. In Great Britain, he limited his appearances to areas other than London, where Maskelyne and Cooke's Egyptian Hall was the center of magic.

In America, while Kellar traveled the world, a few magicians—almost all from Europe—were presenting evening-long stage shows.

Robert Heller (1826?–1878) gained fame as the first magician to perform mind reading in America. Born in England as William Henry Palmer, Heller moved to the United States as a young man. He was a pianist as well as a magician, and he mixed music with magic tricks in his show. Audiences loved his sense of humor. Heller successfully appeared in America and throughout Europe and Asia.

After Heller's death in 1878, Alexander Herrmann (1844–1896) became America's most well-known magician. Herrmann was born to a German family in Paris, France. He began his magic career as a boy assistant to his older brother, magician Carl Herrmann. Alexander established his own reputation during three years of performances at London's Egyptian Hall. In 1874, he brought his show to America.

Herrmann the Great was famous for his exceptional sleight-of-hand skills and his bullet-catching trick. His wife, Adelaide, was his assistant. With his show a major success, he bought a mansion, yacht, and private railcar. After his death in 1896, Herrmann's widow created her own show based on what she had learned from her husband. Adelaide performed until she was in her seventies.

Robert Heller

Alexander Herrmann

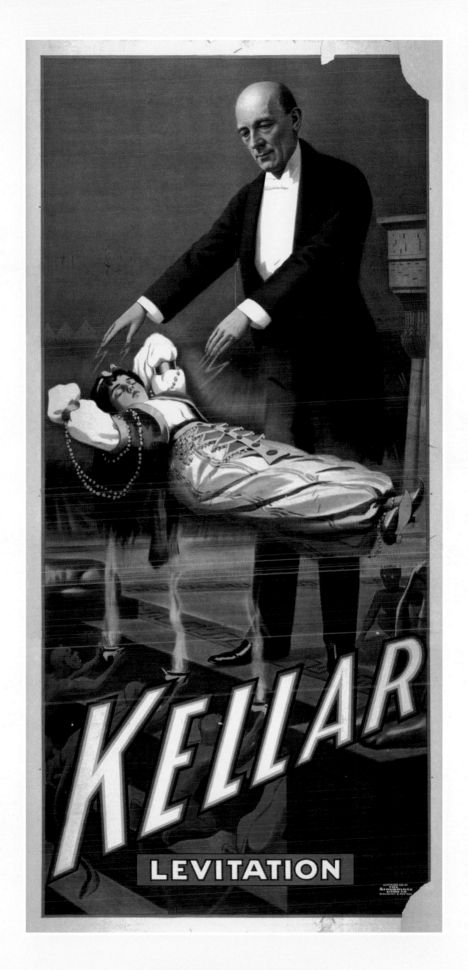

KELLAR'S FAMOUS ILLUSION, 1900

THE QUEEN OF ROSES, 1895

In the Queen of Roses, a woman suddenly appeared out of thin air, surrounded by flowers, in the middle of the stage.
Eva Medley Kellar was the queen.

GROWING ROSES

**"I HOPE TO
BE ABLE
TO GET SOME
FIRST CLASS
THEATRE IN
LONDON
OR NEW YORK
AND SETTLE
DOWN."**

FOR YEARS, Harry dreamed of performing each night at the same theater, the way John Nevil Maskelyne did at the Egyptian Hall in London. He had written his father before leaving on his second world tour: "I hope to be able to get some first class theatre in London or New York and settle down."

In December of 1884, Harry got his chance. A theater with two thousand seats was available in Philadelphia, Pennsylvania, the country's second-largest city at the time. Kellar rented the building for six months and renamed it the Egyptian Hall.

"TEMPLE OF AMUSEMENT"

He advertised his show at the "Temple of Amusement" as being "high-class" and "refined" and "attracting the best audiences in the city." Kellar wore formal evening clothes, looking and acting like a well-mannered gentleman.

His program included the Cabinet Séance and his favorite sleight-of-hand tricks. He made a silk handkerchief vanish from one glass container and reappear in another. In the Spiritual Table Tipping, Kellar floated a table and chair above the stage.

With his automaton Psycho perched onstage, Kellar stepped into the audience and asked a volunteer to donate a coin. The magician didn't appear to look at it. Yet the moment the owner handed over the coin, Psycho displayed number cards showing the coin's date.

Audiences loved the Fairy Flower Trees trick. Kellar placed two empty flowerpots on separate tables. After planting a seed in one pot, he lowered an empty cone over it. When he lifted the cone, a small sprout was growing in the pot.

Then he covered the second pot with the cone. When he raised it a moment later, the audience saw a full-sized blooming rosebush in the pot. Stepping back to the first pot, Kellar covered it with the cone again. When he lifted it, the sprout had grown into a bush full of red roses. Kellar snipped the fresh flowers and passed them out to women in the audience.

The highlight of the two-hour program was his new illusion, the Great Levitation. Kellar stood in the front of the stage, and the theater's gaslights were lowered. His assistant shined a lantern on Kellar. Slowly, the magician's feet lifted from the stage. While the astonished audience watched, he floated to the top of the theater. As he touched down again onstage, the lights came on.

FAIRY FLOWER TREES WINDOW CARD, 1895

Smaller advertising posters like this one were displayed in windows. Throughout his career, Kellar used several different names for his flower-growing trick.

FLYING ABOVE THE AUDIENCE, 1884

This poster for Kellar's Great Levitation was written in both English and Spanish.
It was printed by H. A. Thomas Lithographing Company of New York.

ENTERTAINMENT IN KELLAR'S TIME

During the late nineteenth and early twentieth centuries, people enjoyed concerts, plays, lectures, and other live shows such as magic and vaudeville.

Magic shows were advertised as family entertainment. Conjuring books and pamphlets became popular as amateur magicians of all ages learned to amaze friends. Harry Kellar wrote several magazine articles explaining how to do simple tricks at home.

Vaudeville shows included eight or more short acts by singers, dancers, comedians, and magicians. Unlike vaudeville magicians, Harry Kellar toured as the featured performer in his own two-hour show. Vaudeville's popularity grew until the 1920s, when motion pictures took over.

Traveling circuses also attracted crowds. Two of the best known were The Barnum and Bailey Greatest Show on Earth and Buffalo Bill's Wild West.

[TOP]
The Barnum and Bailey Circus, 1897
The attractions of P. T. Barnum (1810–1891) first became popular in the 1840s. Later he went into the circus business. In 1881, Barnum and circus manager James A. Bailey (1847–1906) formed the circus eventually called "The Greatest Show on Earth." The poster was printed by Strobridge Lithographing Company.

[ABOVE]
Buffalo Bill's Wild West, 1899
The poster depicts American Indians attacking pioneers, a battle that was part of the show. William "Buffalo Bill" Cody (1846–1917), shown in the inset, was the star.

54

QUICKER THAN THE EYE

Kellar put on a show every evening and three afternoon matinees a week. Ticket prices ranged from twenty-five cents for a balcony seat to seventy-five cents for a seat on the main floor. At that price, people from all walks of life could afford to come and bring their children.

Crowds soon filled Harry's Egyptian Hall Theater. He was thrilled when one special person attended—Isaiah Harris Hughes, the Fakir of Ava. Hughes was impressed by his former assistant's show. So were the critics. One wrote that Kellar's performance was "the best exhibition of magical skill we have ever seen."

Harry had worked hard to improve, becoming a much better magician than he was before his world travels. During his twenty years onstage, he learned that a magician had "only his hands and body to rely upon [as] thousands of eyes fixed upon him, picking flaws."

Although he was naturally right-handed, Harry had trained himself to use both hands with equal skill. His hands and wrists were extraordinarily powerful so that he could do rope escapes. The well-developed muscles in his arms helped him move with unusual speed.

Harry took good care of his body so that it stayed strong and limber. He ate healthy foods. Every morning he exercised and walked several miles.

He improved his mind, too. Harry came up with clever ways to remember facts, details, and every step in an evening's performance. He learned how to rapidly solve difficult math problems and then used that feat in his show.

After a newspaper reviewer criticized him for saying, "I done this trick," Harry concentrated on correcting his poor grammar. He had spent little time in school after age eleven, and his speech didn't fit the polished gentleman he wanted to be.

"THE GREATEST MAGICIAN"

Kellar's successful show continued for nearly three hundred performances. In late June 1885, the Egyptian Hall closed for the summer. Because theaters were uncomfortable during the hot months, many shut down until cooler fall weather arrived.

For the rest of his career, Harry always took his vacation in the summer. He traveled to London's Egyptian Hall to check out the newest magic performances. Then he usually visited his father and brother in Erie, Pennsylvania. Kellar enjoyed children, and he looked forward to spending time with his two nieces and two nephews.

In September, Harry opened the 1885–1886 theater season in Erie's opera house. Erie had prospered as an industrial city, and more than thirty thousand people now lived there. Kellar's hometown was proud of its famous son. Hundreds of his admirers had to be turned away from the packed theater.

"THE BEST EXHIBITION OF MAGICAL SKILL WE HAVE EVER SEEN."

Later that winter, a fire destroyed the Philadelphia theater that had been home to Harry's Egyptian Hall. So instead of staying in one theater for the season, he toured major eastern and midwestern cities.

His advertising notices called Kellar "The greatest Magician in the world; who has mystified and astonished the people of all nations." For a quarter, theatergoers could buy his book, which contained his secrets for fast arithmetic calculations as well as an account of his world tours.

Harry hired musicians to play during intermission. Early in 1887, he added a cornet player named Eva Medley. He had met her five years earlier in Australia, and they had been writing to each other ever since. A talented musician, Eva played solos and operated the cornet-playing automaton Echo. Eventually, she became part of Kellar's illusions. During their tour through Michigan in November 1887, Harry and Eva married.

Despite the success of his show, Harry wasn't able to book the country's biggest theaters. He had competition. While Harry had toured the world, Alexander Herrmann established himself in the United States. Herrmann had acquired many fans since moving from Europe in 1874.

In 1887, one newspaper compared the country's two most celebrated magicians: "As a sleight of hand performer, Mr. Kellar is not superior, or even equal, to Herrmann; but in that his [Kellar's] illusions are more original . . . , he [Kellar] surpasses him measurably."

Determined to be known as "America's Magician," Harry worked harder.

A TRAVELING SHOW

Between the Civil War and 1885, the year that Harry Kellar's show began touring the United States, the miles of railroad track crisscrossing the country quadrupled. Entertainers like Kellar were now able to travel quickly and easily between towns.

Kellar planned his yearly tours to stop at large towns and cities in the Northeast and Midwest, where most Americans lived. By booking theaters along a train route, he could move a dozen or more employees and equipment to a new theater in less than a day. As a result, he made more money in a shorter amount of time. Kellar rarely went to Canada and the West Coast because the trip took too long.

American cities were growing, thanks to an increase in factory jobs and recent immigration from other countries. With so many people looking for entertainment, Kellar usually filled a theater. In big cities, he stayed as long as a month. In smaller towns, where he couldn't sell as many tickets, he performed only one night.

When Kellar's train arrived at the railroad station, horse-drawn wagons met him. They hauled his many cases and trunks full of costumes, curtains, and equipment to the theater. His crew unpacked the show and set up the props and illusions on the stage. After his run ended, Kellar and his troupe headed to the next railroad stop and did it all over again.

[TOP]
Train Travel
Kellar traveled through the United States in a passenger train like this one from 1883—the first train from St. Paul, Minnesota, to Portland, Oregon.

[ABOVE]
Come to the Show
Children and their parents line up to see a live performance at a Massachusetts theater in 1912.

THE WONDERFUL FLY-TO, 1895

Kellar used variations of his Fly-To illusion throughout his career.

FLY-TO

IN LATE March 1889, thirty-nine-year-old Harry Kellar took a walk through a bustling New York City market. He wore a high silk hat and an expensive coat. Harry had invited a newspaper reporter to come along.

Stopping at a vegetable stand, Kellar grabbed one of the bystanders by his coat. "Look here, my man," he said, "you shouldn't do a thing like that." Then he pulled a carrot from the man's pocket.

When the man protested that he hadn't stolen the carrot, Kellar pulled turnips from his other pocket and several potatoes from under his hat. The confused man ran from the scene.

"It's Kellar, the magician!" a voice called. Harry had been recognized. Soon a large crowd gathered.

Strolling through the market, Kellar lifted a second man's hat. Onions fell to the ground. He cut a parsnip in half, and fifteen half-dollar coins poured out. He pulled sausages from a gentleman's coat and coins from a butcher's nose. Kellar even yanked a clucking chicken from under a policeman's uniform.

By the time he left the market, several hundred people were following him, eager to see what magic he would do next. The reporter's newspaper story guaranteed Kellar even more publicity.

COLLECTING SECRETS

Harry did his best to build his reputation and make his show more extraordinary than Alexander Herrmann's. "You can never interest the modern public," he wrote, "unless you are continually giving them something new." People wanted to be mystified, and Kellar knew how to do that.

Each summer, he and Eva traveled to London to collect the most spectacular illusions he could find. Sitting in John Nevil Maskelyne's theater, Harry took notes as he watched the new illusions. He offered to buy the best ones from their creators. If the inventor wouldn't sell the secret—and Maskelyne never would—Kellar found another way.

> "YOU CAN NEVER INTEREST THE MODERN PUBLIC UNLESS YOU ARE CONTINUALLY GIVING THEM SOMETHING NEW."

Harry Kellar convinced his audiences that they were witnessing the impossible: a woman floating above the stage, a man disappearing into thin air, a seed growing instantly into a flower. How did he do it?

His secrets were based on science.

Many of Kellar's tricks and illusions used mechanics. Carefully hidden pulleys, ropes, levers, hinges, wires, and springs shifted and lifted assistants and props.

Some illusions used optics. Stage lighting and the scenery's color and pattern altered the audience's view and camouflaged key elements of the illusion. Precisely placed mirrors made people and objects look as if they were somewhere else—or even invisible.

For several tricks, Kellar took advantage of the chemical properties of certain liquids and gases to produce magical effects.

But science wasn't enough to impress an audience. Much depended on Kellar's performance skills: his smooth, well-timed movements; the drama he created with his patter; and the sly way he directed the spectators' attention away from the secret.

(See more about the science behind magic in the For More Information section, page 90.)

At times, Harry paid off or hired away other magicians' employees who knew the secret to an illusion he wanted. When he found a young magician who was talented at devising new illusions, he made him an assistant.

Harry had a gift for understanding how machines worked. He hired a mechanic, and together they studied other magicians' performances to figure out the science behind each illusion. They often came up with ways to improve it, making it more breathtaking. Then Harry took their design to a company that built magic equipment. Many illusions cost him thousands of dollars to construct.

WEAVING A STORY

The mechanics of a fantastic illusion were only part of its success. Harry's showmanship was what made it memorable. Each illusion had special costumes, stage props, and lighting that would, in his words, "prepare the observer's mind for a mystery though there be no mystery."

Kellar created that mysterious atmosphere with his patter. He knew that Asia was a fascinating and unfamiliar continent to Americans who seldom left their communities. So he embellished his patter by telling audiences that he studied magic in India, "whose magicians have been famous since the time [of] the Egyptian sorcerers."

When Kellar performed his Blue Room, he claimed that Indian fakirs taught him its secret. The illusion began with Eva, dressed in an evening gown, walking into a blue-walled room set up onstage. Eva smiled and waved to the audience. Then slowly, as if melting away, she transformed into Kellar.

He sat down on a chair and waved his hands and arms. Gradually, his body turned into a skeleton waving its arms. The bones separated from the skeleton and floated around the chair. Then, in full view of the audience, the bones reconnected and Kellar reappeared sitting in the chair. "That, Ladies and Gentlemen," he said, "is how we will all look one hundred years from now."

In Yoge's Lamp, Kellar placed an antique lamp on a table. He explained that he borrowed it from an Indian holy man, but he had to return it every night. He wrapped a silk cloth around the lighted lamp. The audience could see its glow through the cloth.

"I shall count three . . . and fire this pistol," Kellar announced. "Instantaneously the atoms composing the lamp will be disintegrated by the force of my will and fly through the fourth dimension of space to India, where they will reassemble and materialize in their former shape." As he fired, the cloth dropped away and the lamp vanished.

EERIE AND EXOTIC

Kellar used unusual names for his illusions and tricks to make them sound eerie and exotic. The Cassadaga Propaganda involved a cabinet that appeared too small to hold a person. Kellar placed the cabinet on a sheet of glass laid between two chairs or stands. A "ghost" inside the cabinet wrote on slates, rang bells, and threw out flowers. When the cabinet was opened, however, it was empty. Harry took the name from Cassadaga Lakes, New York, the site of a spiritualist community.

Eva Kellar's mind-reading act was called Karmos. She sat blindfolded in a chair onstage. Harry walked into the audience, and people showed him objects. Eva named each item. She recited serial numbers on money and identified each card in a deck as it was held up. Audience members gave her complicated math problems, and she instantly solved them.

Kellar ended his program with the illusion Fly-To. The Egyptian princess Karnak was locked inside a cage, and its curtains were drawn. Kellar fired three shots from a pistol. He opened the cage door. *Poof!* Princess Karnak had vanished. Instantly, she reappeared in a matching cage hanging ten feet above the stage. It was as if she had flown to it. The Fly-To finale left audiences shaking their heads in amazement.

As Harry performed each illusion, he cleverly covered up its secret by directing the audience's attention to something else, such as a firing gun or a beautiful girl. He used to say that if he succeeded in distracting an audience, "a brass band playing at full blast can march openly across the stage behind me, followed by a herd of elephants, yet no one will realize that they went by."

ASTARTE ILLUSION, AROUND 1889

At Kellar's command, the magician's assistant Dot Robinson floated above the stage and turned handsprings in midair.

RIVALRY!

Over the next several years, Harry's rivalry with Alexander Herrmann heated up. Harry thought Herrmann was trying to steal his illusions and assistants. When the two magicians performed in the same city, Herrmann's workers pasted his posters over Kellar's. Harry's men did the same thing to Herrmann.

Driven by the intense competition, Harry made his show even better. He, his assistants, and stage crew rehearsed over and over. For an illusion to work, the timing had to be flawless. Every detail was important.

Harry demanded top-notch props and equipment. He hired skilled craftsmen to build them using the finest materials. Before each performance, Harry checked his equipment himself. If a prop didn't work properly or his assistant made a mistake, he lost his temper. But he didn't stay angry for long, and he later apologized for his outburst.

KELLAR

[LEFT]

BUSHY MUSTACHE, 1889

Kellar still had his mustache at age forty.

[RIGHT]

CLEAN-SHAVEN, AROUND 1892

Kellar shaved his mustache when he was about forty-three, because he thought it muffled his voice onstage.

Kellar was satisfied only when the magic was perfect. Once, after a performance, an audience member revealed that he knew how one of the magic boxes worked. Harry pulled the expensive box outside the theater, grabbed an ax, and destroyed it. Then he redesigned a new box so that the trick was impossible to figure out.

Harry expected perfection from himself, too. A critic told him that his bushy mustache muffled his voice and made his onstage patter hard to hear. Harry shaved off the mustache and remained clean-shaven.

By the time Kellar was forty-seven, his fame and reputation had grown in the United States. Alexander Herrmann was known for his sleight-of-hand abilities, but Harry received rave reviews for his illusions. "They are so entirely beyond the imagination," wrote a critic, "that the spectators are left in a condition of hopeless bewilderment."

Then in December 1896, Alexander Herrmann had a fatal heart attack while traveling through New York State by train. From that day on, no magician in America could match Harry Kellar. He became "The Peerless Magician."

THE CASSADAGA PROPAGANDA, 1894

In Kellar's popular Cassadaga Propaganda illusion,
the ghost inside the cabinet popped into an audience member's handkerchief and danced around the stage.

AN EVENING OF MAGIC, 1894

The poster highlights tricks and illusions in Kellar's show, all from his book of magic:
the Spirit Cabinet's flying musical instruments; the dancing handkerchief in the Cassadaga Propaganda;
Eva Kellar and her mind-reading act; and a floating woman.

PRINCESS KARNAC LEVITATES, 1904

When he performed this illusion, Kellar told audiences that he learned its secret in India.
In publicity for the levitation, he changed the spelling of the Fly-To princess's name from *Karnak* to *Karnac*.

THE LEVITATION OF
PRINCESS KARNAC

AFTER MANY years, Kellar's show was polished. Each performance lasted about two and a half hours and included five or six stunning illusions.

Harry's pleasant, friendly personality made him seem like a beloved uncle. Parents who had seen him perform when they were young brought their own children to his shows. He was so famous that his posters required only his name and face. The public instantly identified him as the great magician.

When the popular children's book *The Wonderful Wizard of Oz* was published in 1900, readers recognized the wizard. He looked and acted like the bald, good-natured Kellar— America's real-life wizard.

THE WONDERFUL WIZARD OF OZ

This illustration of the Wizard of Oz by W. W. Denslow appeared in the original book, published in 1900, by L. Frank Baum. To many readers, the character resembled Harry Kellar, the most famous American magician at the time.

"Exactly so! I am a humbug"

Harry toured throughout the United States every September through May. He performed his show as many as ten times a week. Then he spent the summer months planning and preparing for the next theater season.

Whenever their grueling schedule allowed, Harry and Eva returned to their home overlooking the Hudson River outside of New York City. They regularly visited Erie, Pennsylvania. Harry's father had died in 1894, but his brother, Eduard, still lived there. Sometimes Harry gave a performance in an Erie theater.

"GRANDEST OF ALL MYSTERIES"

An important part of every year was Kellar's annual summer trip to London's Egyptian Hall. One year he watched Maskelyne do the best levitation he'd ever seen.

Although Kellar already performed a levitation, he wanted something more baffling and unforgettable. He attended many shows at Egyptian Hall and studied the stage carefully, but he couldn't figure out the details of Maskelyne's levitation. Maskelyne refused to reveal its secret.

Harry's solution was to hire someone who knew how the illusion worked. A German magician, Paul Valadon, had performed at Egyptian Hall for five years. In 1904, Kellar invited Valadon to join his show.

After Valadon described the mechanism behind the illusion, Harry made changes to it. Unlike Maskelyne, who performed every night in the same theater, Harry had to move the illusion as he toured. That meant adjusting the equipment so that it could be easily taken down and set up again without breaking.

His ingeniously redesigned illusion filled nine large, heavy trunks when it was packed for traveling. In each new theater, stagehands spent several hours setting up the wires, winches, and cables that made the illusion work.

But that was all behind the scenes. When Kellar presented the Levitation of Princess Karnac to audiences, he wove an enchanting mystery. He told how he had seen a Hindu magician perform a levitation in India six years before. The magician wouldn't reveal how it was done. So Kellar followed the man and "discovered the secret of this grandest of all mysteries."

THE WITCH, THE SAILOR AND THE ENCHANTED MONKEY, 1905

The poster shows the magic play's seven characters, with Harry Kellar and his imp friends looking on.

The beautiful Princess Karnac lay on a couch in the center of the lighted stage. Kellar moved his hands above her as if putting her in a trance. Gradually, she rose from the couch into the air. When she was as high as his head, assistants slid the couch away.

Kellar walked around and under her. He passed a metal hoop around her body once, then twice, to prove that no wires or stand held her up. Kellar let audience members examine the hoop to confirm that it was solid, with no gaps. After Princess Karnac hovered in midair for about ten minutes, the couch was moved back and she slowly floated down again.

Audiences were astounded. The critics were impressed. "His levitation this season," said one newspaper review, "is the most mystifying and marvelous mechanical illusion ever accomplished by a magician."

Even though the illusion was based on Maskelyne's invention, Harry had improved the method. From then on, it was called "Kellar's Levitation" in America.

THE WITCH, THE SAILOR AND THE ENCHANTED MONKEY

The next season, Paul Valadon suggested an addition to the show. The Witch, the Sailor and the Enchanted Monkey was a humorous magic play in which Valadon had a role when he worked at Egyptian Hall. It combined several illusions that Harry had used before.

A wooden cabinet served as a jail cell. Kellar invited volunteers to come onstage to examine it for trapdoors. Nobody ever saw a way to escape the cabinet.

The play began with a sailor arrested and locked in the jail. His girlfriend begged the witch (Kellar) to release him. Using magic, the witch made the sailor disappear. A monkey (an assistant in costume) appeared in the sailor's place. Seven characters continued to dramatically vanish and reappear. After thirty minutes, the play ended with the sailor back in jail.

The illusion was a hit. One newspaper reported: "He [Kellar] is a source of keen delight to the youngsters . . . as well as to the children of larger growth."

Paul Valadon expected to inherit the Kellar show when fifty-eight-year-old Harry decided to retire. But after three seasons, at the end of the 1906–1907 tour, Kellar changed his mind about Valadon. The reason, some of Harry's employees later claimed, was because Eva Kellar disliked Valadon and his wife. Others said Harry was concerned that Valadon drank too much alcohol.

Kellar had traveled the globe for most of his life. He was almost ready to stay in one place and relax. But the curtain hadn't closed quite yet.

THE GOLDEN BUTTERFLY, 1906

Kellar introduced this illusion with a story about brilliantly colored butterflies that came to an Indian valley every year.
If a man captured the golden butterfly queen, he would own all of the money in the world.
When the curtains opened, a yellow-and-purple case stood center stage. Kellar waved his hands over it.
Slowly, golden wings unfolded, revealing a woman dressed as a butterfly. When Kellar reached for her, the butterfly vanished.

MRS. KELLAR, 1900

Eva Kellar's Karmos mind-reading performance was popular.
One reviewer wrote: "Her mathematical calculations, her feats of memory, her accuracy and alertness while blindfolded,
are a marvellous performance of mental power."

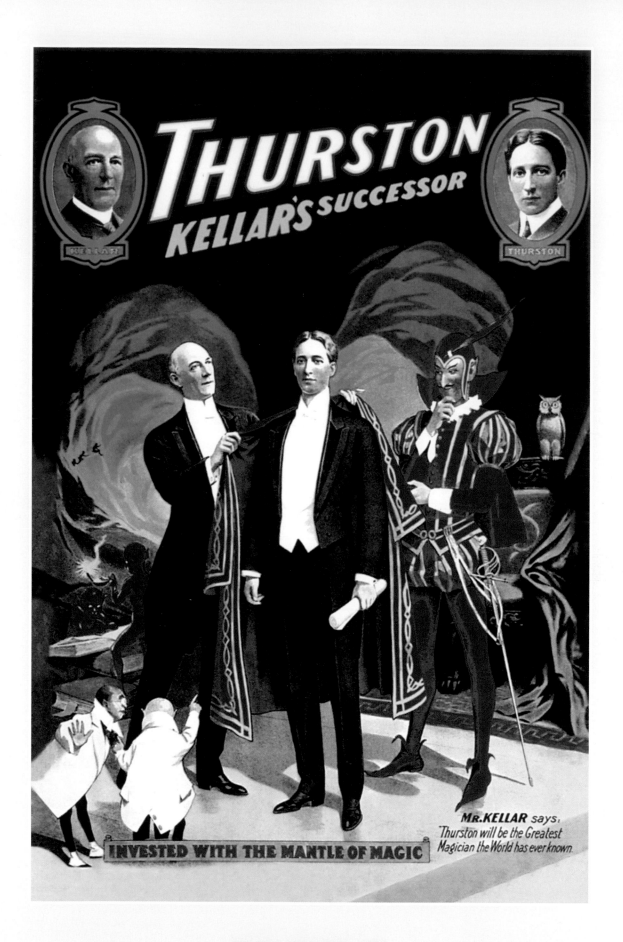

KELLAR'S SUCCESSOR, 1908

This poster publicized Harry Kellar passing his show on to Howard Thurston.
In fact, neither magician wore a cape, and Kellar never draped a cape over Thurston's shoulders.

THE FINAL BOW

IN AUGUST 1907, Harry made a deal to sell his show to Howard Thurston, a younger magician he had met a few years before. He admired Thurston's skill and trusted him to carry on his show. The two agreed that after one final season, Kellar would turn over his illusions, equipment, and costumes.

Kellar and Thurston appeared together throughout the 1907–1908 season. They advertised their show as Kellar's farewell tour. That sold out the theaters.

On May 16, 1908, in Baltimore, Maryland, Harry Kellar gave his final professional performance. At the end of the evening, he announced that Thurston would be his successor. After nearly fifty years of performing magic, Kellar stepped off the stage and out of the limelight.

KELLAR'S NEW HOME

Harry Kellar lived in this house in Los Angeles.

RETIREMENT

Harry was a smart businessman, careful with his earnings. He had saved enough money for a comfortable retirement. He and Eva moved to Los Angeles, California, where the weather was mild. Harry liked fishing in the ocean and driving to the nearby mountains in his expensive car.

HOWARD THURSTON, 1908

Thurston (1869–1936)
was born in Columbus, Ohio.
He made his name in magic
as the King of Cards,
because he was so skilled
with his hands.
Later he expanded
into illusions.
After taking over from
Harry Kellar,
Thurston had a popular show
for twenty-eight years
until his death from a stroke.
The poster reminded
the public that he was Kellar's
hand-picked successor.

In March 1910, soon after they settled into their new house, Eva suffered a fatal heart attack. Harry was devastated.

After Eva's sudden death, Harry's niece and her husband came to live with him in California. Other family members from Erie often visited. He especially enjoyed the long stays of his two great-nieces.

Kellar remained active in the magic world. In his home workshop, he tinkered with tricks and illusions. Determined to improve the levitation illusion, he built a better version, even though he knew he would never use it onstage himself.

Harry wrote letters encouraging other magicians and attended their performances. Each year he made a cross-country train trip back East to see family and magician friends.

Kellar was beloved by his fellow conjurers. To show their respect, many stopped by his house when they came to Los Angeles. They called Kellar the dean of American magicians. Eventually, in 1921, the Society of American Magicians officially named him the first Dean of the S.A.M., the highest honor the organization bestows.

HOUDINI

One of Kellar's admirers was Harry Houdini, who had become famous for his thrilling escapes. Houdini and Kellar developed a close friendship, writing frequent letters to each other. When Houdini was in Los Angeles starring in silent movies, the two men talked for hours about magic. Kellar invested in Houdini's film company and gave him business and personal advice.

One day Harry heard that Houdini planned to perform the Bullet-Catching trick. A magician they both knew well had recently been shot in the chest when the trick went wrong. The man died.

Harry Houdini visited
Ira Davenport at his home in
Mayville, New York,
the year before Ira died.
Houdini respected
the Davenport brothers
as masters of rope escapes.
In 1917, Houdini sent
a copy of this photo to Kellar
with the inscription:

"To my very good friend,
who is an honor
to the magicians art[,]
Harry Kellar[,] and who
is historically our greatest
American magician

Best wishes
from Harry Houdini"

Kellar wrote to Houdini: "This is advice from the heart. DON'T TRY THE D——N Bullet Catching trick. . . . Please, Harry, listen to your old friend Kellar who loves you as his son and don't do it." Houdini followed Kellar's advice.

It was Houdini who convinced Harry to go back on the stage at the age of sixty-eight. In the fall of 1917, during World War I, a German torpedo sunk the U.S. military ship *Antilles* in the Atlantic Ocean. Dozens of men died. To raise money for the families, the Society of American Magicians organized a magic show in New York City. Houdini was the group's president, and he asked Harry to appear.

In the Hippodrome Theatre on November 11, 1917, Kellar once again stepped before a crowd of several thousand. He performed selections from his legendary program, including the Spirit Cabinet. Houdini acted as his assistant. It was the last time the public would see the Great Harry Kellar onstage.

"He is just as good as ever," wrote one reporter, "and works with the same rare skill that made him not only the dean of magicians, but one of the most finished performers we have ever known."

After Kellar took his bow, the other magicians carried him around the stage while the audience applauded. Harry was touched. Three days later, he wrote Houdini, "I shall look back to that grand farewell performance . . . as one of the happiest events in my whole life."

THE SOCIETY OF AMERICAN MAGICIANS

*I*n 1902, two dozen magicians came together in the Martinka brothers' magic shop in New York City and started the Society of American Magicians. Today S.A.M. has thousands of members all over the world and is the oldest magic society. Professional and amateur magicians share tricks, discuss magic techniques, and give performances.

In 1921, the group officially named Harry Kellar the first Dean of American Magicians. The dean is respected by fellow magicians for his skills and his contributions to the art of magic. Only nine magicians have been honored as dean, a title held for life (see For More Information section, page 91).

Other major magician organizations include the International Brotherhood of Magicians and The Magic Circle.

Martinka Magic Shop
The Martinka brothers started their New York City magic shop in the late 1870s. It became a gathering place for conjurers. The company sold magic equipment and built illusions for many magicians, including Kellar. It is still in business and has a shop in New Jersey.

THE CURTAIN CLOSES

Over the next few years, Harry continued to live a relaxing life. In the house he built after Eva's death, he surrounded himself with memorabilia, including magic equipment and autographed photos of celebrities he had met. Always skilled in languages, he studied to improve his French. He drove his car hundreds of miles each week, taking his friends on trips throughout California and Nevada.

When Houdini asked Kellar if he could write the older magician's biography, Harry agreed to share dozens of personal letters and stories with his friend. Houdini interviewed Kellar and wrote part of the book, but he never finished it.

Gradually, Harry's health deteriorated as he suffered a series of illnesses. In late February 1922, he developed pneumonia. On March 10, at the age of seventy-two, Harry Kellar died in Los Angeles.

Magician friends served as pallbearers at his funeral. National newspapers and magicians' monthly bulletins commemorated Harry and his accomplishments.

Kellar had spent his life enchanting audiences who entered his magical world. Presidents, kings, queens, and emperors fell under his spell. Traveling the globe, he dazzled millions of people on six continents and became America's first homegrown magician to gain international fame. Fellow magicians have held him in high esteem for more than one hundred years.

Near the end of his career, Harry's hometown newspaper in Erie paid him this tribute: "It is safe to say that no man living has done more to make this dull world forget its cares and lose its sorrows and its worries than the wizard Kellar."

"IT IS SAFE TO SAY THAT NO MAN LIVING HAS DONE MORE TO MAKE THIS DULL WORLD FORGET ITS CARES AND LOSE ITS SORROWS AND ITS WORRIES THAN THE WIZARD KELLAR."

[RIGHT]
HARRY KELLAR AND HIS DOG

[OPPOSITE]
GOING FOR A RIDE

Harry Kellar enjoyed his cars.
This is his third Cadillac.

Timeline

1849	JULY 11—Born as Heinrich (Henry) Keller in Erie, Pennsylvania.
1860	Runs away from home.
1861–65	**American Civil War.**
1862–67	Works as assistant to the Fakir of Ava.
1865	Performs first solo show.
1867–69	Changes his name from *Henry* to *Harry*; tours Midwest as a solo act.
1869	**Transcontinental Railroad completed.**
1869–73	Works as assistant to Davenport Brothers.
1870–1910	**More than twenty million immigrants come to the United States.**
1873–75	Tours Cuba, Mexico, Central America, and South America with William Fay.
1875	JULY—Performs for Brazil's Dom Pedro II (emperor, ruled 1841–89).
	AUGUST—Loses savings in shipwreck off France.
1875–78	Travels on first world tour as star of the Royal Illusionists.
1876	SUMMER—Changes his name from *Keller* to *Kellar*.
1879–84	Travels on second world tour with the Royal Illusionists.
1879	JUNE—Performs for Brazil's Dom Pedro II.
1880	APRIL—Performs at private estate of Great Britain's Queen Victoria (ruled 1837–1901).
1882	Meets Eva Medley in Melbourne, Australia.
1884–1908	Tours throughout the United States as star of his own show.
1887	NOVEMBER—Marries Eva Medley in Michigan; she joins his show.
1896	DECEMBER—Alexander Herrmann dies; Kellar becomes America's best-known magician.

1898	Spanish-American War.
1904	JANUARY—Performs for President Theodore Roosevelt (in office 1901–09).
1907	AUGUST—Agrees to sell his show to Howard Thurston in Spring 1908.
1908	MAY 16—Gives final professional performance in Baltimore, Maryland, before retiring to California.
1910	MARCH—Eva Medley Kellar dies in Los Angeles, California.
1914–18	World War I.
1917	APRIL—U.S. enters World War I.
	NOVEMBER 11—Makes last stage appearance, at New York City benefit show for families of war casualties.
1922	MARCH 10—Dies at age seventy-two in Los Angeles.

Source Notes

The source of each quotation in this book is found below. The citation indicates the first words of the quotation and its document source. The sources are listed in the bibliography.

The following abbreviations are used:
HK Harry Kellar, *A Magician's Tour, Up and Down and Round About the Earth: Being the Life and Adventures of the American Nostradamus, Harry Kellar*.
WONDERS Mike Caveney and Bill Miesel, *Kellar's Wonders*.

THE WIZARD CASTS HIS SPELL
page 14
"Papa, I didn't . . .": quoted in the *New York Times*, January 18, 1904.
"Would you like . . .": same as above.
"You shall have . . .": same as above.
"Shucks . . .": same as above.

THE OPENING TRICK
page 18
"that the drug . . .": HK, p. 12.
"Every American . . .": *Pittsburgh Gazette*, September 6, 1902, quoted in WONDERS, p. 354.
"got the urge . . .": quoted in Christopher, *Illustrated History of Magic*, p. 199.
"wanted liberty . . .": HK, p. 12.
"Every other boy . . ." and "Come in . . .": quoted in Kellar, "The Wizard at His Tricks," p. 1254.

THE MAGICIAN'S APPRENTICE
page 24
"one of my best . . .": HK, p. 14.
"Look in your . . .": quoted in Kellar, "The Wizard at His Tricks," p. 1255.

"IN LEAGUE WITH THE DEVIL"
page 30
"in league . . .": quoted in HK, p. 32.
"was good enough . . .": HK, p. 22.
"eating fire": HK, p. 38.

"I have been . . .": letter from Kellar to father, April 6, 1875, quoted in WONDERS, pp. 45–46.
"I am too feeble . . .": letter from Kellar to father, August 1875, quoted in Christopher, *The Illustrated History of Magic*, p. 207.

THE FLYING CAGE
page 36
"There is only . . .": letter from Kellar to father, June 25, 1876, quoted in WONDERS, p. 56.
"just to know . . .": same as above.
"I do not think . . .": letter from Kellar to father, June 1877, quoted in WONDERS, p. 67.
"I must fulfill . . .": letter from Kellar to father, October 30, 1877, quoted in WONDERS, p. 72.
"Bravo . . .": quoted in HK, p. 128.
"I have trapped . . .": quoted in Evans, *The Old and the New Magic*, p. 250.
"If you have two . . .": same as above.

PSYCHO
page 42
"It is with genuine . . .": letter from Kellar to Harry Houdini, May 12, 1919, quoted in WONDERS, p. 505.
"Should I succeed . . .": letter from Kellar to father, January 14, 1879, quoted in WONDERS, p. 90.
"There is no one . . .": *Blackpool (England) Gazette & News*, August 10, 1880, quoted in WONDERS, p. 105.
"Their entertainment . . .": *Evening Post* (Wellington, New Zealand), November 18, 1882.
"The repeated applause . . .": *Hong Kong Telegraph*, August 27, 1883, quoted in WONDERS, pp. 119–20.
"The speedy manner . . .": *Free Press* (Queenstown, South Africa), March 17, 1881, quoted in WONDERS, p. 108.
"Gifted with a . . .": *Japan Daily Mail*, September 13, 1883, quoted in WONDERS, p. 121.

GROWING ROSES
page 50
"I hope to be . . . ": letter from Kellar to father, July 25, 1878, quoted in WONDERS, p. 82.

"Temple of Amusement," "high-class," "refined," "attracting . . . ": Kellar advertising letterhead, 1885, in WONDERS, p. 131.

"the best exhibition . . . ": *Turf, Field and Farm*, 1884, quoted in HK, p. 200.

"only his hands . . . ": Kellar, "The Wizard at His Tricks," pp. 1254–55.

"I done this . . . ": quoted by Harry Houdini in "An Editorial by Houdini," in Gibson and Young, p. 238.

"The greatest Magician . . . ": Kellar advertising poster, 1885, in WONDERS, p. 147.

"As a sleight of hand . . . ": *Boston Courier*, June 12, 1887, quoted in WONDERS, p. 155.

FLY-TO
page 58
"Look here . . . ": quoted in *New York Evening Sun*, March 21, 1889, in Cook, p. 208.

"It's Kellar . . . ": quoted in *New York Evening Sun*, March 21, 1889, in Cook, p. 209.

"You can never . . . ": Kellar, "Three Secrets of Success for Every Magician," p. 20.

"prepare the observer's . . . ": Kellar, "Three Secrets of Success for Every Magician," p. 21.

"whose magicians . . . ": Kellar advertising poster, 1895, in WONDERS, p. 297.

"That, Ladies . . . ": quoted in WONDERS, p. 318.

"I shall count . . . ": quoted in Evans, *The Old and the New Magic*, p. 238.

"a brass band . . . ": quoted in Gibson, *The Master Magicians*, p. 99.

"They are so entirely . . . ": *New York Times*, May 28, 1893.

"The Peerless . . . ": Kellar advertising poster, 1898, in WONDERS, p. 327.

THE LEVITATION OF PRINCESS KARNAC
page 66
"discovered the secret . . . ": quoted in Steinmeyer, *Hiding the Elephant*, p. 176.

"His levitation . . . ": John Northern Hilliard, *Rochester Post Express*, September 30, 1904, quoted in WONDERS, p. 377.

"He [Kellar] is a source . . . ": *Washington Post*, March 18, 1906.

"Her mathematical . . . ": review from May 1897, quoted in Moulton, p. 116.

THE FINAL BOW
page 74
"This is advice . . . ": letter from Harry Kellar to Harry Houdini, 1918, quoted in Christopher, *Houdini*, p. 150.

"He is just as good . . . ": *Sphinx*, December 1917, quoted in WONDERS, p. 498.

"I shall look . . . ": letter from Kellar to Houdini, November 14, 1917, quoted in WONDERS, p. 499.

"To my very good . . . ": inscription by Houdini, June 23, 1917, in Price, p. 446.

"It is safe to say . . . ": *Erie Daily Times*, October 9, 1907, quoted in WONDERS, p. 443.

Bibliography*

Ancestry.com. "New York, 1820–1850 Passenger and Immigration Lists" database. Ancestry.com, 2003.

Ancestry.com. "United States Federal Census" database. Ancestry.com, 2009.

Bates, Samuel P. *History of Erie County, Pennsylvania*. Chicago: Warner, Beers, 1884.

Baum, L. Frank. *The Annotated Wizard of Oz*. Centennial ed. Edited by Michael Patrick Hearn. New York: W. W. Norton, 2000.

Caveney, Mike. "Harry Kellar, An American Institution." *Magic*, December 2003, 68–73.

———. "The Rise of Harry Kellar." *Magic*, November 2003, 59–63.

Caveney, Mike, and Bill Miesel. *Kellar's Wonders*. Pasadena, CA: Mike Caveney's Magic Words, 2003.

Christopher, Milbourne. *Houdini: The Untold Story*. New York: Thomas Y. Crowell, 1969.

———. *The Illustrated History of Magic*. New York: Thomas Y. Crowell, 1973.

———. *Panorama of Magic*. New York: Dover Publications, 1962.

Cook, James W. *The Arts of Deception: Playing with Fraud in the Age of Barnum*. Cambridge, MA: Harvard University Press, 2001.

Dawes, Edwin A. *The Great Illusionists*. Secaucus, NJ: Chartwell Books, 1979.

Doerflinger, William. *The Magic Catalogue: A Guide to the Wonderful World of Magic*. New York: E. P. Dutton, 1977.

Evans, Henry Ridgely. "Harry Kellar and His Window Cards." *The Linking Ring*, May 1948, 21–24.

———. *History of Conjuring and Magic*. Kenton, OH: International Brotherhood of Magicians, 1928.

———. "In the Magic Circle." *The Open Court*, 1905, Issue 1, 8–20.

———. *The Old and the New Magic*. 2nd ed. Chicago: Open Court Publishing, 1909.

Evening Post (Wellington, New Zealand). "The Royal Illusionists." November 18, 1882.

FamilySearch. "International Genealogical Index" database. The Church of Jesus Christ of Latter-day Saints, 2008. FamilySearch.org.

Gibson, Walter B. *Houdini's Escapes and Magic*. New York: Blue Ribbon Books, 1930.

———. *The Master Magicians: Their Lives and Most Famous Tricks*. Garden City, NY: Doubleday, 1966.

Gibson, Walter B., and Morris N. Young, eds. *Houdini on Magic*. New York: Dover Publications, 1953.

Goldston, Will. *Secrets of Famous Illusionists*. London: John Long, 1933. Reprinted with a foreword by J. C. Cannell. Ann Arbor, MI: Gryphon Books, 1971.

Harry Kellar Folder. McManus-Young Collection. Rare Book and Special Collections Division, Library of Congress, Washington, DC.

Hay, Henry, ed. *Cyclopedia of Magic*. Philadelphia: David McKay, 1949.

Henderson, Mary C. *Broadway Ballyhoo: The American Theater Seen in Posters, Photographs, Magazines, Caricatures, and Programs*. New York: Harry N. Abrams, 1989.

Hopkins, Albert A., ed. *Magic: Stage Illusions and Scientific Diversions, Including Trick Photography*. Introduction by Henry Ridgely Evans. First published 1897 by Munn and Company. New York: Arno Press, 1977.

Houdini, Harry. Collection. Rare Book and Special Collections Division, Library of Congress, Washington, DC.

———. *A Magician among the Spirits*. New York: Harper and Brothers, 1924.

———. *Miracle Mongers and Their Methods*. New York: E. P. Dutton, 1920.

Jastrow, Joseph. "Psychological Notes upon Sleight-of-Hand Experts." *Science*, New Series, May 8, 1896, 685–689.

Kellar, Harry. "Easy Tricks of a Famous Magician." *Ladies' Home Journal*, September 1907, 27; October 1907, 25; November 1907, 27.

———. "How I Do My Tricks." *Ladies' Home Journal*, November 1897, 5.

———. *Kellar's Aids in Arithmetical Calculations, and Professional Tours around the World*. Philadelphia: Dunlap and Clarke, 1885.

———. "Magic of India and Africa." *Travel, Adventure, Sport and Recreation*, April 1893, 461–462.

———. *A Magician's Tour, Up and Down and Round About the Earth: Being the Life and Adventures of the American Nostradamus, Harry Kellar*. Chicago: Donohue, Henneberry, 1890.

———. "Three Secrets of Success for Every Magician." In *Illustrated Magic* by Ottokar Fischer. New York: Macmillan, 1931.

———. "The Wizard at His Tricks." *The Independent*, May 28, 1903, 1254–1259.

Kellar, Prof. H. "High Caste Indian Magic." *North American Review*, January 1893, 75–86.

McManus-Young Collection, Library of Congress, Washington, DC.

Miesel, William P. "Harry Kellar— Master Showman." *Journal of Erie Studies*, Fall 1995, 43–56.

———. "Harry Kellar's Final Performance in Erie." *Journal of Erie Studies*, Spring 2001, 78–94.

———. "Harry Kellar's First Performance in Erie." *Journal of Erie Studies*, Spring 1998, 31–47.

Moulton, H. J. *Houdini's History of Magic in Boston, 1792–1915*. Glenwood, IL: Meyerbooks, 1983.

New York Times. "How Can It Be Explained." May 23, 1893.

———. "Kellar Fools Roosevelts." January 18, 1904.

———. "The Week at the Theatres." May 28, 1893.

Ottaviani, Jim, and Janine Johnston. *Levitation: Physics and Psychology in the Service of Deception*. Ann Arbor, MI: G. T. Labs, 2007.

Price, David. *Magic: A Pictorial History of Conjurers in the Theater*. New York: Cornwall Books, 1985.

Randi, James. *Conjuring*. New York: St. Martin's Press, 1992.

Robenalt, James D. *Linking Rings: William W. Durbin and the Magic and Mystery of America*. Kent, OH: Kent State University Press, 2004.

Roth, Robert A. *Directions and Misdirection in Magic Show Management: Herrmann, Kellar and Thurston in the United States, 1874–1936*. Medford, MA: Tufts University, 1997.

Silverman, Kenneth. *Houdini!!!: The Career of Ehrich Weiss*. New York: HarperCollins, 1996.

Solomon, Matthew. "Up to Date Magic: Theatrical Conjuring and the Trick Film." *Theatre Journal*, December 2006, 595–615.

Steinmeyer, Jim. *The Glorious Deception: The Double Life of William Robinson, aka Chung Ling Soo, the "Marvelous Chinese Conjurer."* New York: Carroll and Graf, 2005.

———. *Hiding the Elephant: How Magicians Invented the Impossible and Learned to Disappear*. New York: Carroll and Graf, 2003.

Washington Post. "Day of Magician Passing." May 18, 1913.

———. "Latest Dramatic News from the Rialto." March 18, 1906.

*Websites active at time of publication

AN EERIE, MAGICAL WORLD,
1897

Kellar's posters were
sometimes filled
with frightening creatures.

For More Information*

In addition to the resources listed in the bibliography, readers may be interested in the following:

BOOKS

Ottaviani, Jim, and Janine Johnston. *Levitation: Physics and Psychology in the Service of Deception*. Ann Arbor, MI: G.T. Labs, 2007.

In graphic novel style, this nonfiction book tells the story of the quest for the perfect levitation illusion. Characters include Harry Kellar, John Nevil Maskelyne, and Howard Thurston. Drawings reveal the secrets behind the magic.

Woog, Adam. *Magicians and Illusionists*. San Diego: Lucent Books, 2000.

Read eight short biographies of nineteenth- and twentieth-century magicians.

WEBSITES

Kellar

Harry Kellar and Harry Houdini by magicpromotionclub. YouTube. youtube.com/watch?v=apOi61uR2jA

Watch the two magicians together in a short film clip.

A Magician's Tour, Up and Down and Round about the Earth by Harry Kellar. American Libraries. archive.org/details/ magicianstourupa00kellrich

Read a digitized version of Kellar's autobiography, published in 1890.

MagicPedia, part of *Genii, The Conjurors' Magazine.* geniimagazine.com/magicpedia/ Vanishing_Bird_Cage

Discover the history of the Vanishing Birdcage trick (Kellar's Flying Cage) and watch a short video of a magician performing the trick.

How to Do Magic Tricks

Illusioneering. illusioneering.org

Magician-scientists demonstrate amazing magic tricks and explain the math and science behind them. Download instructions for each trick.

"Learn Magic" by Wayne Kawamoto. About.com, Magic & Illusion. magic.about.com/od/beginningmagic/ u/learnmagic.htm

Learn to do easy magic tricks by following simple instructions illustrated with photographs.

"Magic." Activity TV. activitytv.com/magic-tricks-for-kids

Magician Ryan Oakes performs fun magic tricks and reveals how to do them. Site includes printable instructions.

Magic, the Science of Illusion. CaliforniaScienCenter, Los Angeles, CA. magicexhibit.org

Tour this online exhibit developed with the help of professional magicians. Discover the science behind illusions and tricks. Download instructions for tricks to do at home, along with explanations of how they work. Site includes lists of websites and books about the science and history of magic.

MAGICIAN ORGANIZATIONS

Society of American Magicians
magicsam.com/pnps.asp

Website includes a list of the S.A.M. deans, including Harry Kellar.

International Brotherhood of Magicians
magician.org

The Magic Circle
themagiccircle.co.uk

MAGIC POSTERS

"How Stone Lithography Works" by Marshall Brain. HowStuffWorks.
howstuffworks.com/arts/artwork/stone-lithography.htm

Photographs and step-by-step explanation show how a skilled craftsman uses stone lithography to create prints.

Magic Poster Collection. Prints and Photographs Online Catalog, Library of Congress.
loc.gov/pictures (Search "Magic Posters")

View digital images of dozens of advertising posters used by magicians from 1879 to 1936.

DVDS

American Mystic: The Magical Life of Harry Kellar. Produced by Lisa and Rich Gensheimer. Main Street Media, 2012.

Documentary explores Kellar's life and the world of magic between the Civil War and the Roaring Twenties.

Grand Illusions: The Story of Magic, Parts One and Two. Produced and directed by Wilson Coneybeare and Mitchell T. Ness. Paragon Productions, 1998.

Find out about the history of magic and great magicians, including Harry Kellar, Alexander Herrmann, John Nevil Maskelyne, and Harry Houdini. The documentary includes interviews and footage of magic performances.

The Illusionist. Written and directed by Neil Burger. Bull's Eye Entertainment, 2006. Rated PG-13.

Watch an award-winning film about a fictional magician in Vienna, Austria, in the early 1900s. The film depicts theaters and stage magic from Kellar's era and shows the popularity of spiritualism. It features sleight-of-hand tricks and stage illusions, many of which Kellar performed. Professional magicians assisted with the production.

Websites active at time of publication

Index

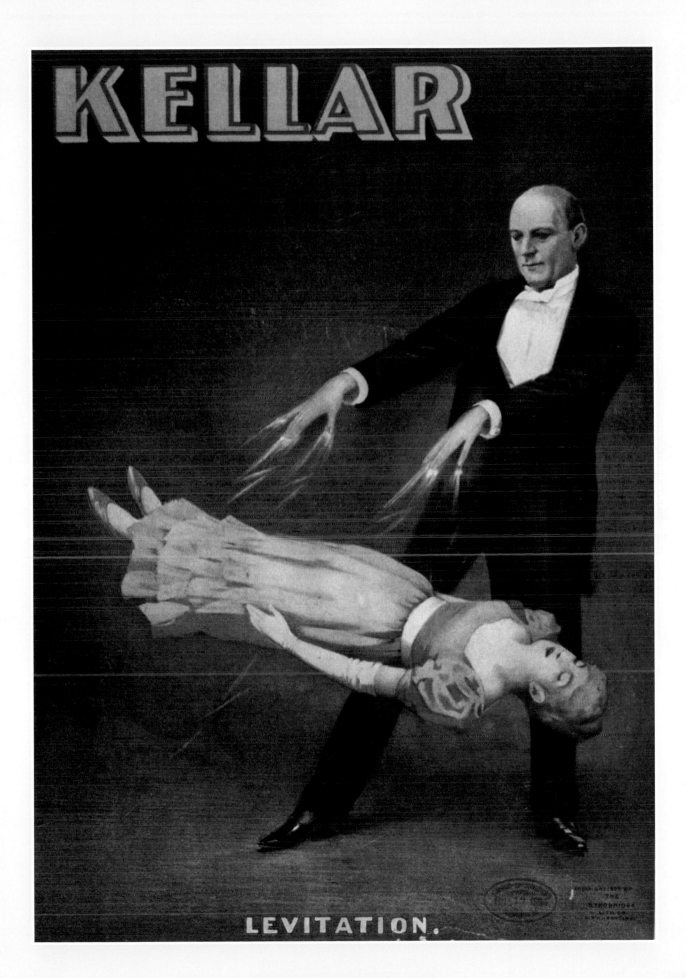

A MYSTERIOUS LEVITATION, 1894

Image Credits